2

The Notebook

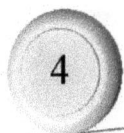

The Notebook

For Me, About Me, By Me

By
Onedia N. Gage, M. Ed.

Other Books by
Onedia Gage, M. Ed., MBA

Are You Ready for 9th Grade . . . Again? A Family's Guide to Success

As We Grow Together Daily Devotional for Expectant Couples

As We Grow Together Prayer Journal for Expectant Couples

The Blue Print: Poetry for the Soul

In Purple Ink: Poetry for the Spirit

Living a Whole Life: Sermons which Prompt, Provoke and Promote Life

Love Letters to God from a Teenage Girl

The Measure of a Woman: The Details of Her Soul

On This Journey Daily Devotional for Young People

On This Journey Prayer Journal for Young People

One Day More Than We Deserve Daily Devotional for the Growing Christian

One Day More Than We Deserve Prayer Journal for the Growing Christian

Promises, Promises: A Christian Novel

Tools for These Times: Timely Sermons for Uncertain Times

With An Anointed Voice: The Power of Prayer

Yielded and Submitted: A Woman's Journey for a Life Dedicated to God

Yielded and Submitted: A Woman's Journey for a Life Dedicated to God Prayers and Journal

Yielded and Submitted: A Woman's Journey for a Life Dedicated to God An Intimate Study

Library of Congress

The Notebook:

For Me, About Me, By Me

All Rights Reserved © 2014

Onedia N. Gage

Purple Ink, Inc. Press

For Information address:
Purple Ink, Inc
P O Box 41232
Houston, TX 77241
www.purpleink.net
www.onediagage.com

ISBN:

978-1-939119-34-6

Printed in United States

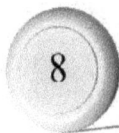

Dedication

Hillary,
when I created this Notebook,
I could not help to get excited about what you would say
And how I would grow from your sharing!
Thank you for being authentic. I value you and admire your spirit!
I love you!

Nehemiah,
I know how much you love to write
And I cannot help but get excited when I know
That I am responsible for that love.
Write so that I may learn and deepen my
Understanding!
I love you!

Dear Student:

I know that your days can seem rough, however there is hope in your future days. You will grow and be exactly what you desire. Right through your youthful storm, it seems that you will not make it out and certainly will not make it out alive. However, every adult has been your age and has had some of these same issues. They have lived through it and have grown from it.

My son just asked me why do I like teaching. I said that I am able to impact lives daily which are filled with drama, hopelessness, harmful activities, and other heartbreaking facts. I have the opportunity to share and give hope in a non-confrontational manner and sometimes a confrontational manner. I live a life which offers a real hope that others are not always willing to share with teens.

Write with the expectation of greatness. I started this notebook because one of my students was having a horrible school year. I thought this would help him to get out his feelings so we could help him reach a resolve. I shared it with my daughter the next day and she loved it so much, she answered the questions within one day. I told her that if she answered these questions every year, the answers would be different. She seemed surprised, as will you.

To the students who this will reach and empower and touch and affect, may these words empower you and help you fervently seek the depths of yourself and reach some resolve. May you be inspired to achieve your goals and dreams. May you enhance your relationship with yourself so that your other relationships will also improve. May you enhance your self-esteem through hard work and study. May you have courage and peace. Share love the best you can until you can share love without reservation.

I look forward to hearing from you about your progress and your successes. You can follow me on twitter @onediagage, email onediagage@purpleink.net, www.purpleink.net, facebook.com/onediagage (education page), blogtalkradio.com/onediagage, http://onediatheeducator.blogspot.com, and youtube.com/onediagage.

I look forward to your success!

Onedia N. Gage

Dear Parent, Teacher, and Administrator:

Greetings Team! You are a team! I greet you as a team because it takes all of us to put the puzzle pieces together to understand the entire puzzle: our student! Each of us has a piece of the whole story. The student needs us to come together to share and SOLVE!

We have the keys to our student's success. They need us to share our experiences and our BOUGHT lessons. I know that they do not listen or do everything we say, however we still need to share. How many times have you been thankful for the one teacher who did not quit on you and invested in you? You are that person because your student is holding this book.

Share transparently and authentically and without reason—not because they did anything to get you to talk. When I share, I remind them that I am human and I am empathetic to their life, with ALL of its drama, ups, downs, changes and excitement. They want to be heard and they need your support. They are assigned to you. They are in your space for a reason—not by accident or happenstance. They BELONG to you!

Listen with an open heart and mind. Treat them like you want to be treated when you have needs and struggles. Give them sound advice without judgment. Although we want them to listen, the answer cannot always be 'no' and 'don't do that.' We do have to let them make some mistakes. We are trying to avoid the detrimental ones and the ones which alter life and cement hopelessness.

Share the great stuff like how did you overcome your hopelessness, homelessness, poverty, abuse, and lack of desire to achieve. Tell them who lifted you with their voice and words of encouragement. Tell them why you are compelled to do the same. Tell them they can succeed even though it looks bleak right now. Show them the way and hold them accountable for that information. Set goals and keep them on track.

Serving them authentically!

Onedia N. Gage
onediatheeducator.blogspot.com ♦ www.purpleink.net ♦ onediagage@purpleink.net ♦ @onediagage

Instructions for Use

Write.
The Notebook was developed to provide you with an avenue of expression. As a classroom teacher, I had a student who was experiencing some difficulties with his life. **The Notebook** was created just for him. You should respond to the questions honestly. Feel free to be transparent.

Share.
Share or don't share. Completely your choice. I find that when we write our feelings down, they are easier to share.

Save.
Save your own life. We need to get to a point of understanding ourselves so that we can function in a controlled environment. We want to respond when we have thought carefully and considered wisely the consequences of our actions. As a student and young person, almost an adult, you need to understand you are in training for the rest of your life. The problem I have is that we do not share those lessons in that manner. If I have the benefit of sharing what I see in store for you down the road, then I can share with you a best practice or method I know of that will help you get there efficiently. I am defining efficiently with the understanding that we are using the path with the least amount of trouble and the easiest way to reach the goal. This means that I am not going to always offer the short cut, yet the best method. Likewise, I want to teach how to make the correct decision in the future.

Time.
The time you spend in this notebook is for you. Use it selfishly and wisely!

The Notebook
For You, About You, By You

15

16

The Nerve to Dream

By Onedia N. Gage

You have the nerve to dream
And expect others to do the same
The audacity

You know dreams don't come true
You know that we don't leave our circumstances
You know that we cannot convince others to believe falsely

You have the nerve and the audacity
To expect us to dream
When there is blight and slums and
Economic hardships

You still dream for better than we have it
Better than all our ancestors
We have more educated
We have more educators
We have more leaders
We have more politicians
We have more wealthy
We have more
. . . yet you still dream of more

You dream that still more can happen
The audacity of you
And the nerve
And the gall of
You to tell our children that they
Can have more than we have
Define more

The Notebook

How much more
More with what?
Less?

Dreams.
You still do it
And in the worst of times
By perception
By the naked eye
But up close they deserve every opportunity to dream
They deserve hopes
They deserve dreams
They deserve the audacity to look at me and
<u>Know</u> that they too can have what we have
And have more of it.

You still dream.

Reprinted from <u>In Purple Ink: Poetry for the Spirit</u> by Onedia Gage

Table of Contents

The
Questions

For Me, About Me, By Me

22

Who are you?

How did you reach that definition?

Are you comfortable with who you are? Why or why not?

_____

_____

_____

_____

_____

_____

_____

_____

_____

_____

_____

_____

_____

_____

_____

_____

_____

_____

_____

How are you defined by others? How do you know?
How did they reach that definition?
Are you comfortable with that definition? Why or why not?
Are you doing anything to change that definition?

_____

_____

_____

_____

_____

_____

_____

_____

_____

_____

_____

_____

_____

_____

_____

_____

_____

What would you change about yourself?
Why is that an important change?
Who supports that change?

_____
_____
_____
_____
_____
_____
_____
_____
_____
_____
_____
_____
_____
_____
_____
_____
_____
_____

What makes you happy?

What happens when you are happy?

_____

_____

_____

_____

_____

_____

_____

_____

_____

_____

_____

_____

_____

_____

_____

_____

_____

What makes you sad?

What happens when you are sad?

_____

_____

_____

_____

_____

_____

_____

_____

_____

_____

_____

_____

_____

_____

_____

_____

_____

_____

_____

_____

What disappoints you?

What happens when you are disappointed?

_____

_____

_____

_____

_____

_____

_____

_____

_____

_____

_____

_____

_____

_____

_____

What excites you?
Who do you share that excitement with?
What do you do when you are excited?

_____

_____

_____

_____

_____

_____

_____

_____

_____

_____

_____

_____

_____

_____

_____

_____

_____

_____

_____

What would you like to be/do as an adult?
Why? Who influenced that decision?

_____

_____

_____

_____

_____

_____

_____

_____

_____

_____

_____

_____

_____

_____

_____

Who influenced who/what you want to be as an adult?

_____
_____
_____
_____
_____
_____
_____
_____
_____
_____
_____
_____
_____
_____
_____
_____
_____
_____
_____

Is your education important to you? Why or why not?

_____

_____

_____

_____

_____

_____

_____

_____

_____

_____

_____

_____

_____

_____

_____

_____

_____

Is your definition of who you are defined by others? Who? Why?

_____
_____
_____
_____
_____
_____
_____
_____
_____
_____
_____
_____
_____
_____
_____
_____
_____
_____
_____
_____

What do you need to be successful?

Who do you need to be successful?

_____

_____

_____

_____

_____

_____

_____

_____

_____

_____

_____

_____

_____

_____

_____

_____

How do you define success?
Who helps you to be successful?

_____

_____

_____

_____

_____

_____

_____

_____

_____

_____

_____

_____

_____

_____

_____

_____

_____

_____

_____

Do you feel successful?
When do you feel successful?

_____

_____

_____

_____

_____

_____

_____

_____

_____

_____

_____

_____

_____

_____

_____

_____

How do you define manhood/womanhood?

Why do you define manhood/womanhood in that manner?

Who helped shaped that definition of manhood/womanhood?

_____

_____

_____

_____

_____

_____

_____

_____

_____

_____

_____

_____

_____

_____

_____

_____

_____

_____

_____

_____

What determines your mood each day?

_____

_____

_____

_____

_____

_____

_____

_____

_____

_____

_____

_____

_____

_____

_____

_____

Who/What makes you angry?

What determines how long you stay angry?

What do you do to resolve that anger?

_____

_____

_____

_____

_____

_____

_____

_____

_____

_____

_____

_____

_____

_____

_____

_____

_____

How do you feel about your education?

What makes your education important to you?

What makes you want to succeed in your education?

_____

_____

_____

_____

_____

_____

_____

_____

_____

_____

_____

_____

_____

_____

_____

_____

How do you feel about your family?

Why?

Is there a particular event that caused these feelings?

_____

_____

_____

_____

_____

_____

_____

_____

_____

_____

_____

_____

_____

_____

_____

_____

_____

How does your family feel about you?
Why? Is there a particular event that caused these feelings?

_____

_____

_____

_____

_____

_____

_____

_____

_____

_____

_____

_____

_____

_____

_____

_____

How is your family defined? Feel free to draw a picture, if desired.

_____

_____

_____

_____

_____

_____

_____

_____

_____

_____

_____

_____

_____

_____

_____

_____

_____

_____

How do you feel about your family structure/dynamics?

_____
_____
_____
_____
_____
_____
_____
_____
_____
_____
_____
_____
_____
_____
_____
_____
_____

If you could pick your family, would you pick the one you have? Why?
If not, who would you pick as a family? Why?

_____

_____

_____

_____

_____

_____

_____

_____

_____

_____

_____

_____

_____

_____

_____

_____

_____

_____

_____

What are important family values for you?
Are these currently functioning in your home?

_____
_____
_____
_____
_____
_____
_____
_____
_____
_____
_____
_____
_____
_____
_____
_____

What should a family do and be?

_____

_____

_____

_____

_____

_____

_____

_____

_____

_____

_____

_____

_____

_____

_____

_____

_____

_____

The Notebook

Are rich and poor important to you? How do you define rich and poor? Are you rich or poor?
Do you let rich/poor define who you are?

_____

_____

_____

_____

_____

_____

_____

_____

_____

_____

_____

_____

_____

_____

_____

_____

What is your family legacy?

Consider family education, businesses owned, homeownership, and overall activities.

_____

_____

_____

_____

_____

_____

_____

_____

_____

_____

_____

_____

_____

_____

_____

_____

_____

_____

The Notebook

Have you learned well enough to help your future children with their homework?

_____

_____

_____

_____

_____

_____

_____

_____

_____

_____

_____

_____

_____

_____

_____

_____

_____

Do you feel that you are smart?
Why or why not?
Does this affect how you feel about yourself?

_____
_____
_____
_____
_____
_____
_____
_____
_____
_____
_____
_____
_____
_____
_____
_____
_____
_____
_____

Does money motivate you?
Why or why not?
What do you define as "a lot" or "enough" money?
How did you get to that definition?

_____

_____

_____

_____

_____

_____

_____

_____

_____

_____

_____

_____

_____

_____

_____

Who would do you with $100,000?

Who would you tell first?

Who do you know or know of with this amount of money?

_____

_____

_____

_____

_____

_____

_____

_____

_____

_____

_____

_____

_____

_____

_____

_____

_____

What would you do with $1 million?

Who would you tell first?

Who do you know or know of with this amount of money?

_____

_____

_____

_____

_____

_____

_____

_____

_____

_____

_____

_____

_____

_____

_____

_____

What would you do with $10 million?

Who would you tell first?

Who do you know or know of with that amount of money?

_____

_____

_____

_____

_____

_____

_____

_____

_____

_____

_____

_____

_____

_____

_____

_____

_____

_____

Who do you value?

Why?

_____

_____

_____

_____

_____

_____

_____

_____

_____

_____

_____

_____

_____

_____

_____

_____

What do you value? Why?

_____
_____
_____
_____
_____
_____
_____
_____
_____
_____
_____
_____
_____
_____
_____
_____
_____
_____
_____
_____
_____
_____

Who is your best friend? Why?

Do they feel the same way about you?

_____

_____

_____

_____

_____

_____

_____

_____

_____

_____

_____

_____

_____

_____

_____

What has been the best thing that has ever happened to you?
Why?

_____

_____

_____

_____

_____

_____

_____

_____

_____

_____

_____

_____

_____

_____

_____

_____

_____

_____

What is a close second to the best thing that ever happened to you?
Why?

_____

_____

_____

_____

_____

_____

_____

_____

_____

_____

_____

_____

_____

_____

_____

_____

What is the best thing about your childhood? Why?

_____

_____

_____

_____

_____

_____

_____

_____

_____

_____

_____

_____

_____

_____

_____

_____

_____

_____

_____

_____

_____

What is the worst aspect of your childhood?
Why?

_____

_____

_____

_____

_____

_____

_____

_____

_____

_____

_____

_____

_____

_____

_____

_____

_____

What is the worst thing you have ever experienced?
Who did you share that with?

_____

_____

_____

_____

_____

_____

_____

_____

_____

_____

_____

_____

_____

_____

_____

_____

_____

_____

_____

_____

_____

Have you ever experienced the death of someone close to you in age?
Have you ever experienced the death of someone in your family?
Who? How did it make you feel?

_____

_____

_____

_____

_____

_____

_____

_____

_____

_____

_____

_____

_____

_____

_____

_____

How long did it take you to recover from the death of that person(s)?

How long did it take for you to stop being angry?

_____

_____

_____

_____

_____

_____

_____

_____

_____

_____

_____

_____

_____

_____

_____

_____

_____

Have you ever considered suicide?
What made those thoughts cross your mind?
What made you fail to try?
What made the attempt fail? Why?

_____

_____

_____

_____

_____

_____

_____

_____

_____

_____

_____

_____

_____

Have your friends considered suicide?

What do you say when they tell you?

Do you have someone you can ask for help when this happens for them and for you?

_____

_____

_____

_____

_____

_____

_____

_____

_____

_____

_____

_____

_____

_____

_____

_____

_____

_____

_____

Has your heart ever been broken?
By who?
What did you do to recover?
Has the hurt subsided? Are you healed?
How long did it take to heal?

Have you ever been in love?
How did you feel when you were in love?
How long did it last?
Do you look forward to it happening again?

_____

_____

_____

_____

_____

_____

_____

_____

_____

_____

_____

_____

_____

_____

_____

_____

_____

How do you define love?
Who loves you?
Whom do you love?
Is love important to you?

_____

_____

_____

_____

_____

_____

_____

_____

_____

_____

_____

_____

_____

_____

_____

Who do you wish loved you but you don't think that they do?

Why?

Do they know this?

_____

_____

_____

_____

_____

_____

_____

_____

_____

_____

_____

_____

_____

_____

_____

_____

_____

What is important to you (either material or intangible)?

What can't you live without?

Why?

_____
_____
_____
_____
_____
_____
_____
_____
_____
_____
_____
_____
_____
_____
_____
_____

Who do you define as a great parent?
What are you going to do as a parent when you are one?
What are you NOT going to do as a parent?

_____
_____
_____
_____
_____
_____
_____
_____
_____
_____
_____
_____
_____
_____
_____
_____
_____
_____

Do you have a role model?

Who is it?

How did you select that person as your role model?

Who is your favorite teacher?
Why?

_____

_____

_____

_____

_____

_____

_____

_____

_____

_____

_____

_____

_____

_____

_____

_____

_____

_____

_____

Who is your least favorite teacher?
Why?

_____

_____

_____

_____

_____

_____

_____

_____

_____

_____

_____

_____

_____

_____

_____

_____

_____

_____

What has been your best grade/class?
Why?

_____

_____

_____

_____

_____

_____

_____

_____

_____

_____

_____

_____

_____

_____

_____

_____

_____

_____

What is your best school memory?

Why?

Who did you share that with?

_____

_____

_____

_____

_____

_____

_____

_____

_____

_____

_____

_____

_____

_____

_____

_____

_____

Who is your favorite family member?

Why?

How much time do you spend with him/her?

What kind of activities do you do when you are together?

_____

_____

_____

_____

_____

_____

_____

_____

_____

_____

_____

_____

_____

_____

_____

_____

_____

_____

Who is your favorite actor/actress/tv personality/musician?

Why?

If you met them, what would you say?

How would you want to spend that time?

_____

_____

_____

_____

_____

_____

_____

_____

_____

_____

_____

_____

_____

_____

_____

Do you dream?
Who do you share your dreams with?
Do you write them down?

_____

_____

_____

_____

_____

_____

_____

_____

_____

_____

_____

_____

_____

_____

_____

_____

_____

_____

What do you dream of?

_____

_____

_____

_____

_____

_____

_____

_____

_____

_____

_____

_____

_____

_____

_____

_____

_____

_____

What will it take to pursue those dreams?
Who will help you to pursue them?
Who will encourage you to dream?
Who will encourage you to pursue your dreams?

_____

_____

_____

_____

_____

_____

_____

_____

_____

_____

_____

_____

_____

_____

_____

_____

_____

_____

_____

_____

How do you feel about your current life?

Why?

What can you do to make it better?

_____

_____

_____

_____

_____

_____

_____

_____

_____

_____

_____

_____

_____

_____

_____

_____

Do you go on vacations during holidays and summers?
Where do you go? Where do you want to go?
What do you do when you get there?

_____
_____
_____
_____
_____
_____
_____
_____
_____
_____
_____
_____
_____
_____
_____
_____
_____

What has been your best holiday/summer vacation?

Why?

What did you do?

Who spent that time with you?

_____

_____

_____

_____

_____

_____

_____

_____

_____

_____

_____

_____

_____

_____

_____

_____

Would you ever consider changing your first name when you are an adult?

If so, to what?

Do you like your name?

How did you get it?

What does it mean?

Does it have value to you?

_____

_____

_____

_____

_____

_____

_____

_____

_____

_____

_____

_____

_____

_____

_____

What are your hobbies?

_____

_____

_____

_____

_____

_____

_____

_____

_____

_____

_____

_____

_____

_____

_____

_____

_____

_____

What is your definition of fun?

What is the most fun you have ever had?

_____

_____

_____

_____

_____

_____

_____

_____

_____

_____

_____

_____

_____

_____

_____

_____

_____

Define a gang or clique.
Would you consider joining a gang?
Do you know anyone in a gang?
What would you do if the gang tried to get you to join?

_____

_____

_____

_____

_____

_____

_____

_____

_____

_____

_____

_____

_____

_____

_____

_____

What are your favorite songs?

_____

_____

_____

_____

_____

_____

_____

_____

_____

_____

_____

_____

_____

_____

_____

_____

_____

What are your favorite movies?

_____
_____
_____
_____
_____
_____
_____
_____
_____
_____
_____
_____
_____
_____
_____
_____

What is your favorite holiday?

Why?

What do you do on those days?

_____

_____

_____

_____

_____

_____

_____

_____

_____

_____

_____

_____

_____

_____

_____

_____

_____

Do you write as an escape (like poetry, songs, raps or essays)?
What does this writing do to help you navigate life's journey?

_____

_____

_____

_____

_____

_____

_____

_____

_____

_____

_____

_____

_____

_____

_____

_____

Share something you have written.

Write something you have always wanted to write.

_____

_____

_____

_____

_____

_____

_____

_____

_____

_____

_____

_____

_____

_____

_____

_____

_____

_____

What part of your childhood will you share with your child?
Why?
Will you share your report cards with your child?

_____

_____

_____

_____

_____

_____

_____

_____

_____

_____

_____

_____

_____

_____

_____

_____

Define respect.
Who do you respect?
Who respects you?
Why?

_____

_____

_____

_____

_____

_____

_____

_____

_____

_____

_____

_____

_____

_____

_____

_____

_____

_____

What does it take to earn your respect?
List persons who you respect.

_____

_____

_____

_____

_____

_____

_____

_____

_____

_____

_____

_____

_____

_____

_____

_____

Define forgiveness.
Who have you had to forgive?
Why?
Was it hard?

_____

_____

_____

_____

_____

_____

_____

_____

_____

_____

_____

_____

_____

_____

_____

_____

_____

Is there anyone who you have not forgiven?
Why?

_____

_____

_____

_____

_____

_____

_____

_____

_____

_____

_____

_____

_____

_____

_____

_____

_____

_____

Do you have a religious or spiritual life?
What faith or spiritual practices do you exercise?

_____

_____

_____

_____

_____

_____

_____

_____

_____

_____

_____

_____

_____

_____

_____

_____

_____

Define conflict.
How do you resolve conflict with others?
Is your method healthy?

_____

_____

_____

_____

_____

_____

_____

_____

_____

_____

_____

_____

_____

_____

_____

Have you ever been in trouble/suspended from school?

What happened?

Did that consequence influence you to not do that again?

_____

_____

_____

_____

_____

_____

_____

_____

_____

_____

_____

_____

_____

_____

_____

_____

_____

Have you ever been invited to try drugs?

Have you ever tried drugs?

Do you want to try drugs?

Why?

How did it make you feel?

Why do you feel that you needed to try them?

Who did you share this experience with?

Do you know the long term and harmful effects of drug use?

Do you know of anyone addicted to drugs?

_____

_____

_____

_____

_____

_____

_____

_____

_____

_____

_____

_____

_____

_____

Have you ever been invited to try alcohol?

Have you ever tried alcohol?

Do you want to try alcohol?

Why?

How did it make you feel?

Why do you feel that you needed to try them?

Who did you share this experience with?

Do you know the long term and harmful effects of alcohol use?

Do you know of anyone addicted to alcohol?

_____

_____

_____

_____

_____

_____

_____

_____

_____

_____

_____

_____

_____

Have you ever been invited to try prescription drugs?

Have you ever tried prescription drugs?

Do you want to try prescription drugs?

Why?

How did it make you feel?

Why do you feel that you needed to try them?

Who did you share this experience with?

Do you know the long term and harmful effects of prescription drug use?

Do you know of anyone addicted to prescription drugs?

_____

_____

_____

_____

_____

_____

_____

_____

_____

_____

_____

_____

Sex defined. Where did you learn about sex?

Have you had sex?

How did you decide to have sex?

With whom did you have sex: someone special or someone random?

_____

_____

_____

_____

_____

_____

_____

_____

_____

_____

_____

_____

_____

_____

_____

_____

_____

The Notebook

Do you send/receive nude/almost nude pictures of yourself and your peers?
Do you know that is considered child pornography?
Do you share the pictures you have been sent?
Has any of your nude "selfies" been shared?
How did you feel? Embarrassed?

_____

_____

_____

_____

_____

_____

_____

_____

_____

_____

_____

_____

_____

_____

Do you want to have sex (if you have never)?
Why do you feel the need at this time to have sex?
Are you feeling pressured by your mate to have sex?
Do you feel comfortable and equipped to say no?

_____

_____

_____

_____

_____

_____

_____

_____

_____

_____

_____

_____

_____

_____

_____

_____

_____

Have you ever been sexually abused, raped or molested?
Was it by someone you knew or trusted?
Who did you tell? Did the person you told believe you?
How will you heal from this? Have you told someone you trusted who can help?

_____

_____

_____

_____

_____

_____

_____

_____

_____

_____

_____

_____

_____

_____

_____

Do you have any gay or lesbian friends?

How do you feel about the concept?

Have you ever wondered if that is a choice versus something natural?

Has anyone ever tried to persuade you to engage in the activities that define that label?

_____

_____

_____

_____

_____

_____

_____

_____

_____

_____

_____

_____

_____

_____

_____

Define self-esteem.

Where would yours rate on a scale of 1 to 10?

What can you do to improve your self-esteem?

What can help you to improve your self-esteem?

_____

_____

_____

_____

_____

_____

_____

_____

_____

_____

_____

_____

_____

_____

_____

_____

Have you ever been physically abused by your guardian?

How do you feel about that?

Have you told someone you trust about your situation?

_____

_____

_____

_____

_____

_____

_____

_____

_____

_____

_____

_____

_____

_____

_____

_____

_____

_____

What do you like to eat?

Could you eat healthier?

_____

_____

_____

_____

_____

_____

_____

_____

_____

_____

_____

_____

_____

_____

_____

Are you considered overweight?

What can you do to reduce that weight?

Is your weight affecting how you feel about yourself?

Is your weight affecting how others feel about you and treat you?

_____

_____

_____

_____

_____

_____

_____

_____

_____

_____

_____

_____

_____

_____

_____

_____

_____

_____

Define bullying.
Have you ever been bullied?
Have you ever bullied someone?
What did you do to end the bullying?

_____

_____

_____

_____

_____

_____

_____

_____

_____

_____

_____

_____

_____

_____

_____

Define friendship.
What are the characteristics of a friend?
Are you a great friend?
What can you do to be a better friend?

_____

_____

_____

_____

_____

_____

_____

_____

_____

_____

_____

_____

_____

_____

_____

_____

_____

_____

Describe your best Saturday ever. Past or future.

_____

_____

_____

_____

_____

_____

_____

_____

_____

_____

_____

_____

_____

_____

_____

_____

_____

_____

What will you do beyond high school?
What makes that the best choice for you?
Who supports this choice? Why?
Who disagrees? Why?
How did you reach that decision?

_____

_____

_____

_____

_____

_____

_____

_____

_____

_____

_____

_____

_____

_____

_____

_____

_____

_____

Will you go to college?
Where would you like to attend college?
Who supports your decision?
What will be your major?
What else will you while there?

_____

_____

_____

_____

_____

_____

_____

_____

_____

_____

_____

_____

_____

_____

_____

_____

What branch of the military will you pursue to serve?

Why this branch?

Who supports this choice? Why?

Who disagrees? Why?

Why is the military the best choice?

What will you do while you are there?

What will you do after that?

_____

_____

_____

_____

_____

_____

_____

_____

_____

_____

_____

_____

_____

_____

Who do you trust?
What do you trust them with?
Why?
What would happen to ruin your trust?

_____

_____

_____

_____

_____

_____

_____

_____

_____

_____

_____

_____

_____

_____

_____

How do you start your day?

How do you end the day?

_____

_____

_____

_____

_____

_____

_____

_____

_____

_____

_____

_____

_____

_____

_____

_____

_____

_____

_____

How do you define a day as great or not?

_____

_____

_____

_____

_____

_____

_____

_____

_____

_____

_____

_____

_____

_____

_____

_____

_____

Do you have a pet or want a pet?
What kind of pet do you have/want?
Why did you select this pet?

_____

_____

_____

_____

_____

_____

_____

_____

_____

_____

_____

_____

_____

_____

_____

_____

What do you to calm down after being upset?
Who do you talk to about your issue? Adult? Peer?

_____
_____
_____
_____
_____
_____
_____
_____
_____
_____
_____
_____
_____
_____
_____
_____
_____

What activities interest you at school?
Are you participating in those activities?
What does it take to be involved?

_____
_____
_____
_____
_____
_____
_____
_____
_____
_____
_____
_____
_____
_____
_____
_____
_____
_____

Who would you like to meet who has been a historical figure?
Why?

_____

_____

_____

_____

_____

_____

_____

_____

_____

_____

_____

_____

_____

_____

_____

_____

Where are places you would like to travel as an adult?

_____

_____

_____

_____

_____

_____

_____

_____

_____

_____

_____

_____

_____

_____

_____

_____

_____

_____

_____

What are your goals for your life?
Who knows these goals?
Who is helpful to hold you accountable for not quitting or becoming discouraged?

_____

_____

_____

_____

_____

_____

_____

_____

_____

_____

_____

_____

_____

_____

_____

_____

_____

How do you measure another person's investment in your life?
How do you invite other's (teachers, parents, family, etc.) in your life?

_____

_____

_____

_____

_____

_____

_____

_____

_____

_____

_____

_____

_____

_____

_____

_____

_____

Who do you admire? Why?

_____

_____

_____

_____

_____

_____

_____

_____

_____

_____

_____

_____

_____

_____

_____

_____

_____

_____

How do you feel about your life?
Why?

_____

_____

_____

_____

_____

_____

_____

_____

_____

_____

_____

_____

_____

_____

_____

_____

_____

How many of your friends have divorced parents?
Are your parents divorced?
How do you feel about divorce?

_____

_____

_____

_____

_____

_____

_____

_____

_____

_____

_____

_____

_____

_____

_____

_____

Do you know anyone who is homeless?

Have you and your family ever been homeless?

How do you feel about homelessness?

_____

_____

_____

_____

_____

_____

_____

_____

_____

_____

_____

_____

_____

_____

_____

_____

_____

_____

The Notebook

Do you know anyone in foster care?
Do you know anyone who has been adopted?
How do you think they feel about being adopted?
How would you feel about being adopted?

_____

_____

_____

_____

_____

_____

_____

_____

_____

_____

_____

_____

_____

_____

_____

Reflections

_____
_____
_____
_____
_____
_____
_____
_____
_____
_____
_____
_____
_____
_____
_____
_____
_____

Reflections

_____

_____

_____

_____

_____

_____

_____

_____

_____

_____

_____

_____

_____

_____

_____

_____

_____

Appendix

Goals
> How to create them
> How to reach them

Mission

Vision

Values

Dreams

Goals

goal [gohl] *noun*

the result or achievement toward <u>which</u> effort is directed; aim; end.

The questions that you answer when developing goals are as follows:

1. What do I want to accomplish?
2. When do I want to accomplish this by?
3. Who is going to help me and hold me accountable?
4. What do you do when you do not meet the goals as planned?
5. Who do you share your successes with?

Goals

Goals	By When	Who

Mission Statement

A personal mission statement is based on habit 2 of <u>7 Habits of Highly Effective People</u> called begin with the end in mind. In one's life, the most effective way to begin with the end in mind is to develop a mission statement one that focuses what you want to be in terms of character and what you want to do in reference to contribution of achievements. Writing a mission statement can be the most important activity an individual can take to truly lead one's life.

Victor Hugo once said there is nothing as powerful as an idea whose time has finally come, you may call it a credo, a philosophy, you may call it a purpose statement, it's not as important as to what you call it, no it's how you define your definition. That mission and vision statement is more powerful more significant, more influential, than the baggage of the past, or even the accumulated noise of the present.

What is a mission statement you ask? Personal mission statements based on correct principles are like a personal constitution, the basis for making major, life-directing decisions, the basis for making daily decisions in the midst of the circumstances and emotions that affect our lives.

Your statement may be a few words or several pages, but it is not a "to do" list. It reflects your uniqueness and must speak to you powerfully about the person you are and the person you are becoming.

Why should you write a personal mission statement?

Numerous experts on leadership and personal development emphasize how vital it is for you to craft your own personal vision for your life. Warren Bennis, Stephen Covey, Peter Senge, and others point out that a powerful vision can help you succeed far beyond where you'd be without one. That vision can propel you and inspire those around you to reach their own dreams.

Q: How do I go about creating my Personal Mission Statement?

A: A Mission Statement is defined as having goals and a deadline. This is opposed to the notion that a Mission Statement is just a bunch of flowery, general phrases like, "I will be the best business person I can be."

What should you include when writing a great personal mission statement?

- describe your best characteristics and how you express them
- have specific, measurable outcomes (or goals)
- have a deadline — for example, December 31st 2012, or a year from today.

When Stephen Covey talks about 'mission statement' in this quote he is referring to the articulation of your life purpose. "If you don't set your goals based upon your Mission Statement, you may be climbing the ladder of success only to realize, when you get to the top, you're on the WRONG BUILDING." **Stephen Covey – 7 Habits of Highly Effective People.**

Mission Statement Example – Poor (It's more like a Vision Statement)

"I aspire to start my own business. I want to help others and be a better businesswoman. I will deliver the best food with the highest service levels." Jane

Mission Statement Example – Better

"I will start my business within 3 months and plan to grow it to $500,000 in revenues within a year. Using this success my staff and I will spread the word to local schools and businesses about eco-friendly food production in order that we reach at least 100 people within the same time frame. My purpose will be to massively add value to our local community in measurable ways that have a real impact on people's health now and in the future" Jane

What to do with your Mission Statement?

So now we have a mission we can set a range of goals on the road to achieving your outcomes and dreams. Your values are clarified and should be in line with the goals you want to achieve in life so you should find it easier to make decisions and to do the "right thing" because you can simply ask yourself, "Will this help me achieve my mission?"

You can even put your mission statement in an area where your family or even co-workers will see it. For, a mission statement defines who you are and what you stand for. This lets people see how you think and feel, which in turn, will help them respect, think and act in line with your values too.

Mission Statement

_____

_____

_____

_____

_____

_____

_____

_____

_____

_____

_____

Vision Statement

A personal vision/mission statement is the framework for creating a powerful life.

Your personal vision statement provides the direction necessary to guide the course of your days and the choices you make about your life.

The idea is to craft a broad based idea about your life and what will really make it exciting and fulfilling, that's your life vision.

From the vision, you craft a more focused and action orientated "mission" statement based on "purpose". And finally you get to a list of goals, wishes, desires and needs.

In his book 'The Success Principles', Jack Canfield tells us that in order to create a balanced and successful life; your vision needs to include the following seven areas:

1. work and career
2. finances
3. recreation and free time
4. health and fitness
5. relationships
6. personal goals
7. contribution to the larger community

It does not include the distinctive ways that you intend to accomplish your purpose.

Why Write a Personal Vision Statement?

To express:

- your purpose
- your life's dream
- your core values & beliefs

- what you want for yourself
- what you want to contribute to others
- what you want to be

Characteristics of a Vision Statement:

- Engages your heart & spirit
- Taps into embedded concerns & needs
- Asserts what you want to create
- Is something worth going for
- Provides meaning to the work you do
- Is a little cloudy and grand
- Is simple
- Is a living document
- Provides a starting place from which to get more specificity
- Is based on quality and dedication

Key Elements of a Vision Statement:

- Written down and referred to daily
- Written in present tense, as if it has already been completed
- Includes a variety of activities and time frames
- Filled with descriptive details that anchor it to reality

What Visions Are Not:

- A mission statement: "Why do we exist now?"
- A strategic plan: "How do we plan to get there?"
- A set of objectives: "We will accomplish X by Y time to Z% target audience."

Use these questions to guide your thoughts:

- What are the ten things you most enjoy doing? Be honest. These are the ten things without which your weeks, months, and years would feel incomplete.

- What three things must you do every single day to feel fulfilled in your work?
- What are your five-six most important values?
- Your life has a number of important facets or dimensions, all of which deserve some attention in your personal vision statement.
- Write one important goal for each of them: physical, spiritual, work or career, family, social relationships, financial security, mental improvement and attention, and fun.
- If you never had to work another day in your life, how would you spend your time instead of working?
- When your life is ending, what will you regret not doing, seeing, or achieving?
- What strengths have other people commented on about you and your accomplishments? What strengths do you see in yourself?

Vision Statement

_____

_____

_____

_____

_____

_____

_____

_____

_____

_____

_____

Values Statement

A personal **value** is absolute or relative and ethical value, the assumption of which can be the basis for ethical action. A *value system* is a set of consistent values and measures. A *principle value* is a foundation upon which other values and measures of integrity are based.

Some values are physiologically determined and are normally considered objective, such as a desire to avoid physical pain or to seek pleasure. Other values are considered subjective, vary across individuals and cultures, and are in many ways aligned with belief and belief systems. Types of values include ethical/moral values, doctrinal/ideological (religious, political) values, social values, and aesthetic values. It is debated whether some values that are not clearly physiologically determined, such as altruism, are intrinsic, and whether some, such as acquisitiveness, should be classified as vices or virtues. Values have been studied in various disciplines: anthropology, behavioral economics, business ethics, corporate governance, moral philosophy, political sciences, social psychology, sociology and theology to name a few.

Values can be defined as broad preference concerning appropriate courses of action or outcomes. As such, values reflect a person's sense of right and wrong or what "ought" to be. "Equal rights for all", "Excellence deserves admiration", and "People should be treated with respect and dignity" are representative of values. Values tend to influence attitudes and behavior.

Values Statement

_____

_____

_____

_____

_____

_____

_____

_____

_____

_____

Dreams List

_____

_____

_____

_____

_____

_____

_____

_____

_____

_____

_____

_____

The Notebook

_____

_____

_____

_____

_____

_____

_____

_____

_____

_____

_____

_____

Resources

http://www.usa.gov/Topics/Teens.shtml

http://www.teenink.com/Resources

http://www.parentandteenresources.com/

http://www.hhs.gov/ash/oah/oah-initiatives/teen_pregnancy/

http://www.cdc.gov/teenpregnancy/parents.htm

www.thenationalcampaign.org/**resources**/

http://www.suicidepreventionlifeline.org/

http://www.drugfree.org/

http://kidshealth.org/teen/food_fitness/dieting/obesity.html

http://www.medicalnewstoday.com/articles/268983.php

http://www.jhsph.edu/research/centers-and-institutes/center-for-adolescent-health/_includes/Obesity_Standalone.pdf

The Notebook

156

Acknowledgements

God, thank You for Your plans for me. Thank You for *The Notebook: The Book For Me, About Me, By Me,* and choosing me to complete Your project. I just want to please You, God. Thank You for continuing to anoint me and to invest in me and my gifts, which keep surprising me. Thank You for loving and forgiving me.

Hillary and Nehemiah, thank you for supporting me and my endeavors. Thank you for loving me, especially when I do nothing without a pen and a clipboard, thank you for enduring my late nights, your ideas, the sounding board, the love and the support. Thank you for celebrating our legacy.

To my reading team: Hillary Nicole, Madysen Berry, and Kim Joiner. Thank you for reading and answering the questions and editing those errors and clarifying those unclear areas.

To my prayer partners and to my accountability partners, thank you for the long talks and the powerful prayers and the encouragement.

To the students who this will reach and empower and touch and affect, may these words empower you and help you fervently seek the depths of yourself and reach some resolve. May you be inspired to achieve your goals and dreams. May you enhance your relationship with yourself so that your other relationships will also improve. May you enhance your self-esteem through hard work and study. May you have courage and peace. Share love the best you can until you can share love without reservation.

About the Inquisitive One

The author of these questions was an inquisitive child. And now an adult of the same nature. She seeks to ask you so that you grow and are challenged appropriately.
Do not hesitate to ask her!
@onediagage (twitter) * onediagage@purpleink.net * facebook.com/onediagage
youtube.com/onediagage * blogtalkradio.com/onediagage
www.purpleink.net

SUCCESS COACH ♦ INTERVENTIONIST ♦ MASTER TEACHER
MOTIVATIONAL SPEAKER

To invite Ms. Gage speak at your campus for your students, parents or staff,
Please contact us at
@onediagage (twitter) ♦ onediagage@purpleink.net ♦ facebook.com/onediagage
youtube.com/onediagage ♦ blogtalkradio.com/onediagage ♦ www.purpleink.net
http://onediatheeducator.blogspot.com

Publishing

Do you have a book you want to write, but do not know what to do?
Do you have a book you need to publish but do not know how to start?
Would publishing move your career forward?

Let us help

onediagage@purpleink.net ♦ www.purpleink.net

512.715.4243

www.ingramcontent.com/pod-product-compliance
Lightning Source LLC
Chambersburg PA
CBHW081153270326
41930CB00014B/3140